■SCHOLASTIC
News
Nonfiction Readers

A Chick Grows Up

by
Pam Zollman

Children's Press®
A Division of Scholastic Inc.
New York Toronto London Auckland Sydney
Mexico City New Delhi Hong Kong
Danbury, Connecticut

Consultant: Don Bell
Poultry Specialist (emeritus)
University of California, Riverside

Reading Specialist: Francie Alexander

Photographs © 2005: Charlton Photos/Leigh Charlton: 4 top, 5 bottom right, 16, 17, 21 top right; Corbis Images: 9 (Julie Habel), 5 bottom left, 19 top (Premium Stock), 1 inset, 22 (Garth Webber); Dwight R. Kuhn Photography: cover images, 1, 3, 4 bottom right, 4 bottom left, 5 top left, 8, 10, 11, 12, 13, 14, 15, 20 bottom, 20 center left, 20 top left, 21 center right, 21 bottom, 23 top left, 23 bottom right; Photo Researchers, NY: 2, 5 right, 19 bottom, 20-21 spread (Chris Bjornberg), 23 top right (Tom McHugh), 6, 7 (Will & Deni McIntyre); PictureQuest/Digital Vision: 23 bottom left.

Book Design: Simonsays Design!

Library of Congress Cataloging-in-Publication Data

Zollman, Pam.
  A chick grows up / by Pam Zollman.
     p. cm. – (Scholastic news nonfiction readers)
  Includes bibliographical references and index.
  ISBN 0-516-24944-4 (lib. bdg.)   0-516-24794-8 (pbk.)
  1. Chicks–Juvenile literature. 2. Chickens–Development–Juvenile literature. I. Title. II. Series.
SF487.5.Z65 2005
  636.5'07–dc22

2005002085

R0407133060

CONTENTS

WORD HUNT

Look for these words as you read. They will be in **bold**.

comb

(kohm)

down

(down)

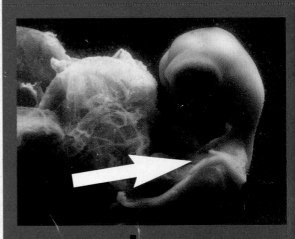

embryo

(**em**-bree-oh)

hatch

(hach)

hen

(hen)

rooster

(**roo**-stur)

wattle

(**wot**-uhl)

5

Peep! Peep!

Did you hear that?

This mother **hen** is with her chicks.

A chick is a bird.

A bird has feathers and lays eggs.

Do you know how a chick grows?

hen

chick

7

A hen lays eggs in a nest.

Some eggs have an **embryo** inside.

An embryo grows into a chick in 21 days.

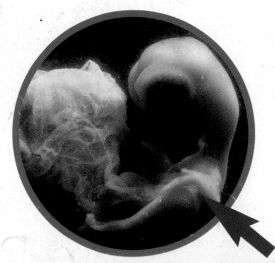

embryo

eggs

This chick wants to **hatch**.

How will it get out?

It cracks open the shell with its egg tooth.

The egg tooth is on the chick's beak.

beak

egg tooth

Look! This chick is hatching.

A chick is wet when it hatches.

A chick has feathers called **down**.

The down will dry fast.

wet down

The chick is almost out of the egg.

Look! The down is dry.

These chicks are dry and fluffy.

They can walk right away.

dry down

Chicks like to eat seeds, bugs, and worms.

15

Chicks grow more feathers in about four weeks.

A **comb** grows on the chick's head.

A **wattle** grows under the chick's beak.

Is this chick grown up yet?

comb

wattle

This chick is
five weeks old.

Chicks are fully grown in six months.

Some chicks grow up to be **roosters**.

Other chicks grow up to be hens.

The hens will lay more eggs.

A rooster is a male, or boy, chicken.

A hen is a female, or girl, chicken.

19

A CHICK GROWS UP!

1···· This embryo is only 10 days old.

2··· The embryo grows into a chick in 21 days. Look! It's hatching.

3···· It can take up to a day for a chick to hatch. Watch it go!

7 Some chicks grow up to be hens, like this one.

6 Watch it grow! It is 5 weeks old.

5 Soon they are dry and fluffy. This chick is 1 day old.

4 Chicks are wet when they hatch. This chick is almost out.

YOUR NEW WORDS

comb (kohm) bright red skin on a chick's head

down (down) the feathers that cover the chick's body

embryo (**em**-bree-oh) a baby that is growing inside an egg

hatch (hach) to break out of an egg

hen (hen) a female, or girl, chicken

rooster (**roo**-stur) a male, or boy, chicken

wattle (**wot**-uhl) bright red skin that hangs under a chick's beak

These Birds Hatch From Eggs, Too!

duck

goose

peacock

turkey

INDEX

FIND OUT MORE
Book:
Face to Face with the Chicken,
by Christian Havard (Charlesbridge Publishing, 2003)

Website: http://www.enchantedlearning.com/subjects/birds/info/chicken/

MEET THE AUTHOR
Pam Zollman is an award-winning author of short stories, articles, and books for kids. She is the author of *North Dakota* (Scholastic/Children's Press®) and the other life cycle books in this series. She lives in rural Pennsylvania where she can watch chicken eggs hatch.